Table of Contents

This book would not have been possible without God and my family, specifically, my elegant wife, Blaire.

I would be remiss if I didn't acknowledge my team and the hard work of my associate, Blake Curtis.

Thank you.

REAL ESTATE AND TAXES: The Tax Guide You Didn't Know You Needed

Byline: Explore the tax implications of buying, selling, and leasing real estate, helping you maximize your tax savings and bolster your compliance with the Internal Revenue Service and state agencies.

Introduction

Did you know that 90% of millionaires in the United States own real estate?[1] How about that 79% of Americans aged 65 and older were homeowners?[2] Real estate is a tried and trusted strategy for building wealth and living the American Dream. As a result, the government incentivizes homeownership through various deductions, credits, and tax advantages. This doesn't mean the government is giving out "free" money. In fact, the IRS and state agencies want their fair share, which comes in the form of different taxes and restrictions.

That's exactly what this book will cover. Throughout this book, we'll dig deep into the tax code, outlining different strategies, limitations, and options you have when it comes to buying and selling real estate. We'll also cover specific situations related to real estate investors and unique situations. Since taxation can widely vary in each state, we'll focus on the tax provisions you need to know at the Federal level. Although many states conform to Federal provisions, slight differences can impact your taxation.

Use this book as your unbiased source to decipher real estate taxation; however, don't place full reliance on the information found in this book. The tax code can change at any time, with countless sections indexed each year for inflation. For the most up-to-date information about a certain section, reach out to our team to schedule your free tax consultation. This book will give you a brief overview of what you need to know, but our team can help you apply these strategies and provisions to your specific situation.

Whether you are a homeowner looking to maximize your deductions or a real estate investor looking for loopholes to lower your tax burden, this book will cover the information you need to know. Let's talk taxes!

---

[1] Spector, Nicole. "90% of Millionaires Are Invested in Real Estate? 5-Steps To Get Started." *Yahoo! Finance,* 17 Oct 2024, https://finance.yahoo.com/news/90-millionaires-invested-real-estate-130127562.html.
[2] Joint Center for Housing Studies of Harvard University. "Housing America's Older Adults." *Joint Center for Housing Studies of Harvard University,* 2023, https://www.jchs.harvard.edu/sites/default/files/reports/files/Harvard_JCHS_Housing_Americas_Older_Adults_2023.pdf.

Part 1: Buying a House

According to the National Association of REALTORS, 4,090,000 existing homes were sold in 2023.[3] Whether you are purchasing a home for your personal use or for investment purposes, there are some tax considerations to keep in mind. We'll start this section by going through the importance of filing income tax returns. In many cases, lenders will use the information reported on your tax return to determine your loan qualification.

Next, we'll move into common tax deductions and tax credits for homebuyers. In these sections, we'll also differentiate which deductions and credits you can take based on the home's primary use. The IRS and state agencies treat personal property differently than business property. Going into these sections, one of the main concepts to understand is the difference between a tax deduction and a tax credit. Tax deductions reduce your taxable income base, while tax credits reduce your tax liability.

Let's look at an example. Your taxable income before any deductions or credits is $50,000, and your average tax rate is 25%. Let's say you qualify for a $10,000 tax deduction. Subtracting $10,000 from $50,000 results in taxable income of $40,000. At a 25% tax rate, your tax liability will be $10,000. Now, let's say that you qualify for a $10,000 tax credit instead of a tax deduction. Your taxable income base will remain at $50,000, creating a tax liability of $12,500. Since tax credits reduce your tax liability dollar-for-dollar, your net tax bill is only $2,500.

Tax credits have a greater impact on your taxes compared to deductions. However, tax deductions are still important to lower your taxable income. Maximizing both tax credits and deductions will result in the most advantageous tax situation.

After our discussion on tax deductions and credits, we'll cover closing costs and their deductibility. In the year you purchase a home, you may need to adjust your deductions to match the timeframe you owned the property. We'll also cover some top tax planning strategies for real estate purchases, such as timing your purchase and leveraging tax-advantaged accounts to hold your investments.

Our final section will cover interest rate implications. Interest rates have remained extremely volatile over the past few years, making it important to understand how changes in rates impact your taxes. Get ready, because this chapter is jam-packed with everything you need to know about purchasing real estate!

The Importance of Filing Income Tax Returns

Purchasing a home can be expensive. Unless you have the funds for an all-cash offer, you will need to seek financing for your home. The good news is that there are countless Federally-backed home-buying programs that allow you to secure fixed rate financing. However, one of the caveats of these programs is meeting rigid qualification criteria. Here are some of the common lender terms you might come across:

---

[3] National Association of REALTORS. "Quick Real Estate Statistics." *National Association of REALTORS,* 7 July 2024, https://www.nar.realtor/research-and-statistics/quick-real-estate-statistics.

- Downpayment Funds– Most lenders require some type of downpayment, which can range from 3% under the First-Time Homebuyer program to 25% for investment property. Some loan programs, such as through the Department of Veterans Affairs, have 0% downpayment programs.
- Debt-to-Income Ratio – A debt-to-income ratio is a comparison of your current debt payments to your average monthly income. When applying for a mortgage, lenders want to see that you'll be able to afford the monthly payment without overextending yourself. Generally, a debt-to-income ratio of 50% or less is ideal.[4]
- Credit Score– Credit score is another important factor. This score measures your history of repaying debts, such as credit cards, student loans, medical bills, car notes, and others. Most lenders require a credit score of 620 or higher; however, certain programs are designed for applicants with a lower score.[5]
- Verified Income – Income is a non-negotiable component of applying for a mortgage. After all, how do you expect to pay your mortgage if you don't have a steady income stream? Lenders want to verify that you are currently employed and earning income.
- Purchase Purpose – Lenders will take a slightly different approach when approving a mortgage for a personal use property versus an investment property.

From a lender's perspective, there is always a risk of fraud when approving a loan application. This is why most lenders default to your income tax returns to verify your income, employment, and work history. For example, if you are purchasing a second investment property, your lender will want to verify the profitability of your first investment property by evaluating your income tax returns. Similarly, a lender will verify your self-employment income or wage earnings by reviewing the income reported on your income tax return.

Since lenders heavily rely on income tax returns for mortgage approval, it's important to report accurate tax returns, especially if you are self-employed. Wiping out all of your income for the year might save you money on taxes; however, it can cause issues when going through the underwriting processes for a mortgage.

Tax Deductions for Home Buyers

Once you've purchased a home, it's important to be aware of potential tax deductions to lower your income tax liability. The deductions you may be eligible for differ based on whether the home is your primary dwelling or an investment property. Let's cover potential tax deductions in each of these categories.

---

[4] Wells, Libby and Segal, Troy. "What is a debt-to-income ratio for a mortgage?" *Bankrate*, 7 June 2024, https://www.bankrate.com/mortgages/why-debt-to-income-matters-in-mortgages/.
[5] US Bank. "What credit score do you need to buy a house?" *US Bank*, 2024, https://www.usbank.com/home-loans/mortgage/first-time-home-buyers/credit-score-for-mortgage.html#:~:text=Credit%20score%20and%20mortgages&text=The%20minimum%20credit%20score%20needed,%2Drate%20mortgages%20(ARMs).

Personal Use Property (Primary Home)

A primary home is also known as your principal residence. This is a property that you live in most of the year. There are a few signs that a house is your primary home. For one, your primary home will be the address to which you send your mail. In addition, your driver's license will list this address, and you will be registered to vote in that county.

For people who split their time evenly between two different homes, you have discretion in which home you list as your primary home. Generally, the home in the state with the most advantageous tax legislation will be picked. For example, if you split your time between Florida and Minnesota, you might elect Florida as your primary residence to take advantage of no state income tax.

Many of the personal use property deductions are found on Schedule A, which is the itemized deduction worksheet. With the Tax Cuts and Jobs Act nearly doubling the standard deduction, many taxpayers no longer itemize their deductions. Here are some Federal tax deductions for personal use property:

- Real Estate Taxes – Property taxes are deductible on Schedule A up to $10,000.
- Mortgage Interest – Interest paid on a primary home loan has no deduction cap on Schedule A. Interest attributed to Home Equity Lines of Credit is deductible if used to build, buy, or improve your residence.
- Home Office Deduction – If you run a business out of a section of your home that is reported on Schedule C or Schedule E, you are able to deduct a portion of your mortgage interest, property taxes, homeowner's insurance, HOA fees, repairs, maintenance, and utilities.
- Mortgage Points – Sometimes, lenders allow you to prepay interest to lower the rate on your loan. These mortgage points are fully deductible on Schedule A in the year you close on the home.

It's important to note that the deductibility of these items at the state level also varies. Some states allow a deduction for these items, while others don't. Consulting with a tax professional is the best way to determine the type of personal use property deductions you can take.

Investment Property (Rentals)

Unlike personal use property, investment property is considered a business according to the IRS. This opens the door to more tax deductions. An expense must be ordinary and necessary to be eligible for deduction. Ordinary means it is common in your industry, while necessary requires the cost to be helpful and appropriate.[6] Here are some examples of eligible investment property tax deductions:

---

[6] Internal Revenue Service. "Tax Guide for Small Businesses." *Internal Revenue Service,* 2 Feb 2024, https://www.irs.gov/pub/irs-pdf/p334.pdf.

- Advertising
- Auto Expenses
- Bank Fees
- Continuing Education
- Contract Labor
- Commissions
- Depreciation
- Homeowner's Dues
- Interest Expense
- Licenses
- Maintenance
- Office Expenses
- Phone Bills
- Professional Fees
- Property Insurance
- Property Management
- Real Estate Taxes
- Repairs
- Software
- Travel
- Utilities

In addition to general business expenses, investment properties have special tax deductions they can leverage to further reduce taxable income. Many of these tax deductions are subject to limitations, making it important to consult with a tax advisor. Nevertheless, here are some common tax deductions real estate investors can take on Schedule E of the 1040:

- Mileage – Traveling from your primary residence or office to a rental property unlocks a mileage deduction. For the 2025 tax year, the deduction is set at $0.70 per mile.
- Section 179 – Section 179 is a special depreciation deduction that allows you to immediately expense the entire cost basis of certain assets in the year placed in service. We'll talk more about this in Part 3.
- Bonus Depreciation – Bonus Depreciation is another special depreciation option put in place by the Tax Cuts and Jobs Act. This provision of the tax code is set to phase out by 2027. We'll touch more on this in Part 3.
- Qualified Business Income Deduction – The Qualified Business Income Deduction is an automatic 20% reduction of your net income (revenue minus expenses). This deduction is also set to expire at the end of 2025 unless an extension of the Tax Cuts and Jobs Act is passed.
- Home Office Deduction – This deduction allows Schedule E filers to write off a portion of their personal housing expenses, as described above.

It's important to note that the above deductions pertain to the individual income tax return. Some real estate investors will form a separate legal entity, such as a partnership or corporation. In these instances, certain deductions are limited. For example, the Home Office Deduction is only available on individual income tax returns. However, this doesn't mean you can't deduct qualifying office expenses. Instead, you may need to set up an Accountable Plan to issue reimbursements.

Working through which deductions you are eligible for as an investor requires extensive knowledge on the tax code, which is why we stress reaching out to an expert. We'll touch more on other real estate tax considerations in Part 3.

Tax Credits for Homebuyers

Homebuyer tax credits are hard to come by. There are only a handful of credits related to real estate that investors and homeowners are able to claim. Let's run through these items in more detail.

Mortgage Interest Credit

This credit is available to anyone issued a qualified Mortgage Credit Certificate by a state or local government agency, which is commonly someone with a lower income. This credit gives you back a portion of the mortgage interest paid during the year. The Mortgage Interest Credit is only available for new mortgages on primary residences.

Energy Efficiency Home Improvement Credit

Over the past few years, the federal government has focused on countless green initiatives. One of these areas was changing the Energy Efficiency Home Improvement Credit.[7] Previously, homeowners could claim a lifetime credit of $500 for energy-efficient upgrades. Now, this credit has been reworked, allowing homeowners to claim the credit each year for qualifying improvements. Here's what qualifies:

- Exterior doors that meet Energy Star requirements – Credit is limited to $250 per door with a maximum of $500.
- Exterior windows and skylights that meet Energy Star requirements – Credit is capped at a maximum of $600.
- Insulation and air sealing materials that meet International Energy Conservation Code standards – Credit is capped at a maximum of $1,200.
- Home energy audits – Credit is capped at a maximum of $150.
- Central air conditioners, water heaters, furnaces, and boilers that meet or exceed the Consortium for Energy Efficiency – Credit is capped at $600 per item.
- Heat pumps, biomass stoves, and biomass boilers that meet or exceed the Consortium for Energy Efficiency – Credit is capped at $2,000 per year.

This credit is calculated at 30% of the item's cost, including labor, up to the maximum. If you're making energy-efficient upgrades, be sure to verify that the item meets the requirements. This credit is claimed on the individual income tax return.

Real Estate Investor Credits

Real estate investors who are running a business may be able to claim other tax credits. Here's a short list of some available credits. Remember, consulting with a tax expert is the best way to determine if you're eligible for these credits. Nevertheless, here are some potential credits to keep in mind:

- Opportunity Zones – In 2017, Congress outlined neighborhood zones that needed development. They incentivized the area to encourage developers to build there. Developers can leverage these credits to eliminate tax on the sale of their development project when building in these zones.
- Historic Tax Credits –Taxpayers who renovate historically significant properties can claim a Federal and state credit of up to 40% of eligible construction costs. The property must be included in the National Register of Historic Places to be eligible for the credit.
- Low Income Housing Tax Credit – The Federal government subsidizes housing in certain areas and for certain tenants. Real estate investors renting to this tenant pool may be eligible for a tax credit.

---

[7] Internal Revenue Service. "Energy Efficient Home Improvement Credit." *Internal Revenue Service,* 13 Nov 2024, https://www.irs.gov/credits-deductions/energy-efficient-home-improvement-credit.

Each of these credits has specific qualification criteria and claiming requirements, making it essential to consult with an expert.

State and Local Credits

In addition to these credits, many states and local jurisdictions offer property tax credits for qualifying residents. These can range from Homestead Credits to Farmland Preservation Credits. Checking with your state agency or contacting an accountant is the best way to determine if you can claim any state tax credits.

Closing Costs and Other Tax Implications

When you close on a new property, you need to pay close attention to the deductions you claim in the first year. This is because certain expenses, like property taxes and prepaid utilities, need to be pro-rated based on your ownership. Looking at an example will be the best way to explain this concept.

Let's say you close on the home on July 1, which is halfway through the year and property taxes aren't paid until December. When you get your real estate bill at the end of the year, you will submit a payment for the full amount. Let's say this amount is $5,000. However, at the time of closing, you likely received a credit for the first half of the year's property taxes. As a result, you can only deduct $2,500 on Schedule A.

To find the credit amount you received, look on your closing statement. Based on the date of the sale, you should have received a credit for unpaid property taxes. If you have any questions about the amount, reach out to your lender or title company, and they should be able to help.

Tax Planning Strategies for Real Estate Purchases

Like most other investment options, there are tax planning strategies you can adopt for your real estate purchases, especially if you are an investor. In this section, we'll run through the importance of understanding the impact of deductions, how to time purchases, and the advantages of leveraging tax-advantaged accounts.

Understand the Impact of Deductions

If you remember our tax deduction section, we discussed different expenses that homeowners and real estate investors can use to lower their taxable income. However, lowering your taxable income can harm your purchasing power. Lenders use your tax return to determine your loan qualification by examining your income sources and the net income you pay taxes on. Writing off too many deductions can reduce your loan qualification amount.

Let's say you have a W-2 job that pays you $100,000 yearly. You also have an existing rental property that generates $500 book cash flow per month, or $6,000 per year. When filing your tax return, you maximize your deductions and report a $5,000 loss on Schedule E. When your lender evaluates your tax return, they will use your net income of $95,000 in the underwriting process instead of your true income of $106,000. Unless you have cash or other investments to pay for your real estate deals, be cautious about taking too many deductions on your tax return.

In addition, Federal and state tax bills are often included in your debt-to-income calculation. Let's say that you consistently owe $5,000 in taxes each year when you file your return. Your lender might actually include this $5,000 in your debt-to-income calculation, lowering your purchase power. To avoid this situation, it's important to make quarterly estimated payments based on your projected income, which a qualified accountant can help you with.

Timing Purchases

Timing your real estate purchases can greatly impact your tax situation. For one, purchasing property can be cash-intensive upfront, especially if you are remodeling or renovating the property. Let's say that your rental business generates $30,000 of taxable income during the year. You decide to purchase a new property and spend $20,000 updating and remodeling the unit. This can potentially reduce your tax bill to $10,000, assuming the improvements qualify for Section 179 and the unit is up and running by year-end.

As a homeowner, you can also leverage renovations and remodels to take advantage of energy-efficient credits. Installing new energy-efficient windows or doors before the end of the year can unlock tax credits to lower your income. Other purchases that might qualify for the energy-efficient credit include furnaces, air conditioner units, insulation, boilers, and water heaters.

Leverage Tax-Advantaged Accounts

One unused tax planning strategy is to hold real estate investments in a tax-advantaged account. Self-Directed Individual Retirement Accounts (IRAs) can hold real estate investments, like rental properties. There are a handful of conditions that must be met to purchase real estate in your IRA, including:

- The IRA is self-directed, meaning the custodian allows alternative investments.
- All transaction paperwork and documentation flow through a custodian.
- The property being purchased is purely for investment purposes. Vacation homes, second homes, and any other personal use property are disqualified.
- Your IRA must pay all expenses. You can't pay for part of the property using funds outside of the IRA.
- No real estate deductions can be taken since the income generated from the property is tax-free.

It's important to note that the custodian of your IRA does not manage your real estate investment. Instead, they handle the back-office paperwork and ensure your investment is compliant with regulations. It's up to you to handle your rental property's management and tax reporting.

Purchasing a property through an IRA should only be done if you have a large balance in the account. Since the IRS limits annual contributions, if you run out of funds to pay for expenses or repairs, you will be penalized for over-contributing. Additionally, you will not be able to leverage real estate tax deductions since the income earned is tax-free. To determine if this strategy is right for your situation, work with an accountant to determine which tax situation is more favorable.[8]

Interest Rate Implications for Buyers

Interest rates play a major role in the financing of your real estate property. In this section, we'll cover the impact of interest rates on your deductions, your refinance, and your purchasing power.

Deductions

Mortgage interest is one of the top deductions for homeowners and real estate investors. When you take out financing on a property, your monthly payment will consist of two components: principal and interest. The principal is the portion of your payment that goes toward your beginning loan balance, while interest goes to your lender. Higher interest rates result in larger mortgage interest deductions, which can be beneficial to help lower your taxable income.

Let's look at an example. You take out a $200,000 mortgage with a 7% interest rate. In the first year, you will pay $13,936 in interest, which can either be deducted on Schedule A if the property is your primary residence or Schedule E if the property is for investment purposes. Over the life of the loan, you will pay $279,018 in interest, assuming no early payments.

Now, let's say that you take out a $200,000 loan at a 5% interest rate. In the first year, the total mortgage interest paid drops to $9,933, resulting in a lower tax deduction. However, over the life of your loan, you are only paying $186,512 in interest. Although you are getting a lower deduction on your tax return, you are saving money in interest over the course of 30 years.

Refinancing

Most homeowners and investors prefer to save more money over the life of the loan rather than have a higher tax deduction. As interest rates go down, you may decide to refinance your mortgage. If you do decide to refinance your mortgage, you may be able to buy down points. If you remember back to our tax deduction section, you can deduct the cost of prepaid mortgage interest on Schedule A in the year of the refinance. It's important to note that the closing costs associated with the refinance are not tax-deductible unless the property is held for investment use.

Purchasing Power

Interest rates also have a direct impact on your purchasing power. Using our above example, a $200,000 mortgage at a 7% interest rate would have a monthly mortgage payment of $1,331, excluding any amounts held in escrow. With a 5% interest rate, this monthly payment drops to $1,074. This is a $257 difference in monthly payments. As interest rates drop, your purchasing power increases, allowing you to buy more expensive properties. Instead of only qualifying for a $200,000 property, maybe you now qualify for a $250,000 property.

However, this doesn't mean that you should look for more expensive properties. This same situation unfolded during the 2008 Mortgage Crisis. As lenders loosened their underwriting criteria,

---

[8] Internal Revenue Service. "Publication 590-A (2023), Contributions to Individual Retirement Arrangements (IRAs)." *Internal Revenue Service*, 9 Sept 2024, https://www.irs.gov/publications/p590a.

more homeowners were eligible to purchase property. Lenders then repackaged these mortgages into pools and sold them to investors. The increase in demand drove housing prices higher. When the housing bubble burst, home prices dropped, leaving homeowners with mortgages that exceeded the fair value of the home.[9]

Although lending criteria have tightened since the 2008 Mortgage Crisis, it is still important to be aware of the debt you are taking on. Higher purchase prices often increase your property taxes and insurance, causing higher prices in more areas than your mortgage payment. Evaluating what you can truly afford, whether you are an investor or a homeowner, is important before purchasing a property.

Conclusion

In this chapter, we covered everything you need to know about purchasing a property, from potential tax deductions and credits to tax planning strategies and interest rate considerations. However, purchasing a property is only half the equation. Most people purchase numerous properties throughout their lifetime. The next section will cover the fundamentals of selling a property, helping you understand what you can expect from a tax standpoint and strategies to lower your tax bill.

Part 2: Selling a House

Selling a home can be plagued with stress and uncertainty. Whether market conditions are less than ideal, buyers won't stop negotiating, or the IRS is knocking on your door for their share, selling a home is anything but easy. This makes it no surprise that Moverly found that 83% of home sellers in a one-year period experienced at least one health issue stemming from stress.[10]

Before we get into what this part will cover, we want to touch on the importance of building your team. Too often, people believe they can sell their homes themselves to pocket more money. This is far from true! The right team on your side eliminates countless stressful situations and has a deep understanding of the process to unlock higher purchase prices and lower taxes.

Your team should consist of at least two professionals: a realtor and an accountant. Your realtor will handle everything about your home sale, including taking listing photos, responding to interested buyers, and helping you select the right offer. Accountants handle all things related to tax return reporting, including reporting the sale on your tax return, minimizing your tax liability, and providing transparency into which type of sale might be best.

Even with these two professionals on your side, it's important to know the tax implications of selling real estate. In this section, we'll cover common types of selling expenses and how these costs can help you lower your tax bill. Then, we'll break down capital gains taxes, including the differences between short-term and long-term capital gains.

---

[9] Federal Reserve History. "Subprime Mortgage Crisis." *Federal Reserve History,* 22 Nov 2013, https://www.federalreservehistory.org/essays/subprime-mortgage-crisis.
[10] Russell, Brandon. "83% of home sellers experience stress related health problems." *IFA Magazine,* 18 Mar 2023, https://ifamagazine.com/83-of-home-sellers-experience-stress-related-health-problems/.

Our next section will cover the tax implications of selling investment property, including the three main taxes you'll see. After we outline the different taxes, we'll jump into tax planning strategies you can apply to your real estate sale to lower your tax liability. We'll end this section with a short discussion on the impact of interest rates on your home sale. Get ready because this section is jam-packed with everything you need to know about selling real estate!

Selling Expenses

Before we get into the type of taxes you can expect when selling real estate, let's first cover selling expenses. Selling expenses are added to your basis, which is your total investment in the property. We'll cover how to calculate your basis in the next section. Here's a short list of costs you might come across when selling your home and their deductibility:

- Real Estate Agent Commissions – Commissions paid to real estate professionals are included in your basis, lowering the amount of potential taxes.
- Real Estate Property Taxes – Some jurisdictions require you to pay any outstanding property tax bills before closing. These are not added to your basis but instead are deducted on Schedule A for homeowners or Schedule E for real estate investors.
- Legal and Title Fees – Like commissions, these expenses are added to your basis when you sell a property.
- Repairs and Home Improvements – Major improvements that you have sufficient documentation for can be included in your basis. For example, replacing the roof prior to closing. Other limits come into play when you claim depreciation on these home improvements.
- Other Professional Fees – Land surveys, consultants, and other professional fees can be added to your basis when you sell.

It's important to keep track of each of the above items when you sell a property. In many cases, your closing statement will outline these factors. Your accountant will request this document when reporting the sale, so keep it handy.

Capital Gains Tax Basics

Have you ever heard the words "capital gains tax" being thrown around in conversations about real estate? This type of tax might sound like a scary concept; however, it can actually result in tax savings. Capital gains tax is a special type of tax imposed on capital assets. The IRS considers everything from personal-use items and household furniture to stocks, bonds, real estate, and businesses as capital assets.[11] The IRS taxes the difference between the sale price and your basis in the capital asset at specific rates based on your income. Let's explore the fundamentals of capital gains taxes in more detail.

Calculating Your Basis

Your basis describes your investment in a capital asset. It includes the upfront costs associated with acquiring the asset. Let's say you bought your home for $300,000. You put $50,000 of repairs

---

[11] Internal Revenue Service. "Topic no. 409, Capital gains and losses." *Internal Revenue Service,* 2 Jan 2025, https://www.irs.gov/taxtopics/tc409.

into the property. This creates a basis of $350,000. When calculating the basis of your primary residence, you need to be careful. You can't deduct a ladder you purchased three years ago and used at your house. Only major repairs and upgrades that you have documentation for should be included in your basis.

Basis gets more complex when you have a rental property since you most likely have taken depreciation. Your basis in a rental property will net depreciation against your investment. For example, if you purchased a property for $250,000 and took $25,000 of depreciation, your net basis is $225,000. In situations where you took depreciation, you may be subject to depreciation recapture, which we'll discuss in a later section. It's also important to note that homeowners who have claimed the home office deduction and depreciated their primary residence may also be subject to depreciation recapture.

Short-Term Vs Long-Term Capital Gains Tax

There are two types of capital gains: short-term and long-term. Short-term capital gains are taxed at ordinary income tax rates, while long-term capital gains are subject to special rates. A short-term capital gain occurs when you purchase and sell the same capital asset within a 12-month period. Here are the Federal marginal tax brackets for the 2025 tax year:[12]

2025 TAX RATE	SINGLE	MARRIED FILING JOINTLY	MARRIED FILING SEPARATELY	HEAD OF HOUSEHOLD
10%	$0 to $11,925	$0 to $23,850	$0 to $11,925	$0 to $17,000
12%	$11,926 to $48,475	$23,851 to $96,950	$11,926 to $48,475	$17,001 to $64,850
22%	$48,476 to $103,350	$96,951 to $206,700	$48,476 to $103,350	$64,851 to $103,350
24%	$103,351 to $197,300	$206,701 to $394,600	$103,351 to $197,300	$103,351 to $197,300
32%	$197,301 to $250,525	$394,601 to $501,050	$197,301 to $250,525	$197,301 to $250,500
35%	$250,526 to $626,350	$501,051 to $751,600	$250,526 to $375,800	$250,501 to $626,350
37%	$626,351 or more	$751,601 or more	$375,801 or more	$626,351 or more

Long-term capital gains rates go into effect when you hold onto the property for more than one year. The long-term capital gains tax rate your income is subject to depends on your taxable

---

[12] Parys, Sabrina. "2024 and 2025 Tax Brackets and Federal Income Tax Rates." *NerdWallet*, 2 Jan 2025, https://www.nerdwallet.com/article/taxes/federal-income-tax-brackets.

income. Here are the rates and the income levels based on each filing status for the 2025 tax year:[13]

FILING STATUS	0% RATE	15% RATE	20% RATE
SINGLE	< $48,350	$48,351 to $533,400	> $533,401
MARRIED FILING JOINT	< $96,700	$96,701 to $600,050	>$600,051
HEAD OF HOUSEHOLD	<$64,750	$64,751 to $566,700	>$566,701

Comparing the two tables, it's clear that long-term capital gains tax rates have the potential to lower tax liability. Unlocking these favorable tax rates is a top planning strategy that we'll discuss in more detail in our Tax Planning section.

Handling Capital Losses

There is no limit on the amount of capital gains subject to taxation; however, the IRS does limit the losses you can take. Capital losses are capped at a deduction of $3,000 each year ($1,500 for married filing separately) on the individual income tax return.[14] Any losses in excess of $3,000 are carried forward indefinitely to offset future gains.

Remember, capital losses can be used to offset capital gains. Let's say that you had $50,000 in capital gains. In the same year, you also had $75,000 in capital losses. As a result, your net capital loss is $25,000. In the current year, you will be able to claim $3,000 in losses, with the remaining $22,000 carried forward to future years. It's also important to note that the sources of capital gains and losses do not matter when it comes to offsetting. You could use a loss from the sale of an investment property to offset a gain on a stock you sold during the year.

Homeowner Exclusion

Homeowners can take another exemption to reduce their capital gains tax, known as the Section 121 exclusion. This exclusion allows single taxpayers to reduce their capital gains by $250,000. Married filing joint taxpayers are eligible for a $500,000 deduction. To qualify, you must meet two tests: a use test and an ownership test. These tests require that you have used the home as your primary residence for at least two out of the prior five years. The five-year period is extended to ten years for individuals on qualified official extended duty in the Uniformed Services.[15]

Let's say that you purchased your home for $300,000 and it sells for $500,000. You file a joint return and meet the use and ownership tests. Under normal capital gains regulations, you would owe tax on the $200,000 gain. However, since you lived in the home for at least two years and filed a joint return, you are able to eliminate up to $500,000 of capital gains. It's important to note that any

---

[13] Taylor, Kelley. "IRS Updates Capital Gains Tax Thresholds for 2025." *Kiplinger,* 7 Nov 24, https://www.kiplinger.com/taxes/new-irs-long-term-capital-gains-tax-thresholds.

[14] Internal Revenue Service. "Topic no. 409, Capital gains and losses." *Internal Revenue Service,* 2 Jan 2025, https://www.irs.gov/taxtopics/tc409.

[15] Internal Revenue Service. "Topic no. 701, Sale of your home." *Internal Revenue Service,* 27 Sep 2024, https://www.irs.gov/taxtopics/tc701.

excess exclusion remains unused and cannot offset other gains or be carried forward. In this situation, the $300,000 of excess exclusion goes unused.

Another implication of the homeowner exclusion appears when you depreciate the property. If you've depreciated a portion of your home, you cannot exclude that portion and you will need to recapture depreciation. Using our above example, let's say you claimed $25,000 in depreciation. You will pay no capital gains tax on the sale, but you will need to pay depreciation recapture on the $25,000. We'll talk more about depreciation recapture in the next section.

Tax Implications of Selling Investment Property

Selling your primary home is relatively simple from a tax perspective, even with depreciation recapture. This isn't the case for selling investment property. Here are the three types of taxes you may be subject to when selling investment property.

Capital Gains

We touched on capital gains tax in the previous section. This is the most common tax that real estate investors pay when selling a property. Remember, capital gains tax rates only apply to long-term capital gains. If you buy and sell a property within a 12-month period, you will likely pay ordinary income taxes at your marginal rate.

Depreciation Recapture

The next type of tax when selling an investment property is depreciation recapture. As a refresher, depreciation is the reduction of an asset's cost basis over the useful life. Depreciation can also come in the form of special depreciation options that allow for a larger upfront deduction in the year placed in service. Since depreciation reduced your taxable income in prior years, the IRS requires you to pay taxes on the amount taken.

Let's say that you sold a lawnmower used in your real estate business for $500. In the prior year, you expensed the entire asset's cost basis of $2,500. As a result, your net basis is zero and your taxable gain is $500. Depreciation recapture on Section 1245 and Section 1250 is taxed at ordinary income rates, which generally trend higher compared to capital gains tax rates. The amount of your gain subject to depreciation recapture is based on the smaller of your realized gain or your total depreciation expense.

Net Investment Income Tax

The Net Investment Income Tax (NIIT) is a 3.8% tax imposed on certain investments, like interest, dividends, and capital gains. If your rental property was a passive activity, gains may also be subject to NIIT. NIIT is applicable when your modified adjusted gross income exceeds $200,000 if single or head of household or $250,000 if filing joint.[16]

Let's say your adjusted gross income was $300,000 as a single taxpayer. In the current year, you sold a property that generated $20,000 of capital gains. Since you are above the threshold, your

---

[16] Internal Revenue Service. "Topic no. 559, Net investment income tax." *Internal Revenue Service*, 2 Jan 2025, https://www.irs.gov/taxtopics/tc559.

$20,000 gain will also be subject to NIIT, assuming it was a qualifying passive activity. Now, let's say that your gain was $150,000. Subtracting the $200,000 threshold from your $300,000 adjusted gross income results in only $100,000 of your gain being subject to NIIT.

Reporting the Sale on Your Tax Return

Although you might not owe taxes on the sale of your property, you do still need to report the information on your income tax return. The tax return reporting for real estate sales will differ based on the type of sale. For example, an investment property would be reported on a separate form compared to the sale of your personal home. We'll cover the specific reporting criteria of each sale type next. However, before we do so, let's cover the three main documents you will need to report your real estate sale.

- 1099-S – Form 1099-S outlines important information about the property sale, including the closing date, the gross proceeds, pro-rated real estate taxes, your residency status, and if you received property or services as part of the consideration.[17] This form is reported to the IRS, meaning the information reported on your tax return should match the 1099-S. Form 1099-S is only issued to the seller of the property. Below is a snippet of the form.

		CORRECTED (if checked)		
FILER'S name, street address, city or town, state or province, country, ZIP or foreign postal code, and telephone number		1 Date of closing	OMB No. 1545-0997	
			Form **1099-S**	**Proceeds From Real Estate Transactions**
		2 Gross proceeds	(Rev. April 2025)	
			For calendar year	
		$		
FILER'S TIN	TRANSFEROR'S TIN	3 Address (including city, state, and ZIP code) or legal description		**Copy B** **For Transferor**
TRANSFEROR'S name				This is important tax information and is being furnished to the IRS. If you are required to file a return, a negligence penalty or other sanction may be imposed on you if this item is required to be reported and the IRS determines that it has not been reported.
Street address (including apt. no.)		4 Transferor received or will receive property or services as part of the consideration (if checked) . . . . ☐		
City or town, state or province, country, and ZIP or foreign postal code		5 If checked, transferor is a foreign person (nonresident alien, foreign partnership, foreign estate, or foreign trust) . . . . ☐		
Account number (see instructions)		6 Buyer's part of real estate tax		
		$		

Form **1099-S** (Rev. 4-2025) (keep for your records) www.irs.gov/Form1099S Department of the Treasury - Internal Revenue Service

- Closing Statement – A closing statement is a detailed list of the transactions related to the sale. Items such as real estate commissions, title charges, pro-rated real estate taxes, other professional fees, the gross sale price, your loan payoff amount, and the cash due to you upon closing will be reported here. This information is crucial for reporting the sale on your tax return. If you remember back to our Selling Expenses section, many of the charges on your closing statement can increase your basis and lower your tax liability.

---

[17] Internal Revenue Service. "About Form 1099-S, Proceeds from Real Estate Transactions." *Internal Revenue Service,* 11 Sep 2024, https://www.irs.gov/forms-pubs/about-form-1099-s.

- <u>Bank Statement</u> – Any time you receive proceeds from the sale, it's important to double-check that the amount deposited into your bank account matches your closing statement. This quick double-check can save you a headache down the road with the IRS.

You will need each of these forms to report the sale on your tax return accurately. Now, let's cover the specific reporting criteria for sales of primary homes and investment property.

Reporting Your Primary Home Sale

The sale of your primary home will be reported on Schedule D only if you have a taxable gain. You won't need to report the sale on your tax return if you qualify for the homeowner exclusion. However, most tax software comes with supplementary schedules that aren't sent to the IRS. Providing your home sale information to your accountant will populate this schedule with your return to ensure correctness.

Let's say that you sold your home for $500,000. You meet the requirements for the homeowner exclusion, and you originally purchased the property for $300,000. As a result, the $200,000 calculated gain is not taxable and will not show on Schedule D. Instead, you might find the transaction information on a separate schedule that is not sent to the IRS. Now, let's say that you don't qualify for the homeowner exclusion. The $200,000 taxable gain will populate on Schedule D.

Reporting Your Investment Property Sale

Investment property sales are also found on Schedule D. However, unlike the sale of your primary home, both gains and losses will populate on this form. Let's say that you purchase an investment property for $200,000. The market drops, and you end up selling the property for $175,000. Excluding any additional basis items, you will report a $25,000 loss on Schedule D.

Moreover, investment properties can be subject to depreciation recapture, which is calculated on Form 4797.[18] Similarly, if you decide to sell your investment property through an installment sale, you will also need to fill out Form 6252. Form 6252 is required for each year the installment sale is active. For example, if you enter into an agreement to sell your property over 15 years, you will need to attach Form 6252 to your return for the next 15 years. We'll cover installment sales in more detail in the next section.

Tax Planning Strategies for Real Estate Sales

Just like there are tax planning strategies for buying a house, there are also strategic options for selling a house. In this section, we'll outline the main tax planning strategies for timing your real estate sales, helping you minimize your tax liability.

Timing Sales

The timing of your home sale matters. For one, the homeowner exclusion requires that you live in your primary home for two out of the past five years. If you are under the two-year mark and are thinking of selling your home, consider waiting until you satisfy this requirement. Remember, the

---

[18] Internal Revenue Service. "Instructions for Form 4797 (2023)." *Internal Revenue Service,* 17 Jan 2024, https://www.irs.gov/instructions/i4797.

homeowner exclusion only applies to excess gains over your basis (up to $250,000 for single filers and $500,000 for joint filers). If you expect a loss from the sale, you do not need to take this exclusion. As a reminder, losses are not deductible when they relate to your primary home.

Even if you satisfy the requirements for the homeowner exclusion, you want to be strategic about your home sale. Data shows that the best time to sell a house is in June. Listing your home for sale in early spring gives you access to a larger buyer pool, which creates competition for your listing and can drive up your sale price. Additionally, be aware of local market conditions. If your area is experiencing job growth and lenders offer mortgage incentives, it might be a good time to sell your home.

Although the small details of selling your home aren't as important as the economy's overall health, Zillow research has found that the best day to list your home is Thursday. Homes listed on Sundays tend to sit on the market longer compared to those listed on Thursdays. Even more surprising, Thursday listings were more likely to sell over the asking price. As you pursue the sale of your home, consider asking your agent to list on a Thursday![19]

Many of these considerations also apply to real estate investors. You want to be aware of when you are listing your house, including the month and the day of the week. However, real estate investors also have other factors to keep in mind. First, understand your property type and the expected buyer. If you are listing a rental property with an expiring lease, it might be beneficial to fill the vacancy before you list it for sale. Buying an unoccupied property adds risk for the buyer. Taking the initiative and filling the vacancy before listing can help you maximize your sale price.

Similarly, real estate investors need to be cognizant of their other sales during the year. If you remember back to our capital gains tax section, we talked about how the capital gains rate you pay taxes on depends on your income. If you are nearing the threshold for the next bracket, you may want to hold off on the sale of another investment property until the next year. Working with a tax accountant will be important to understand where your income falls year-to-date and what that means for your real estate sales.

1031 Exchanges

1031 exchanges, also known as like-kind exchanges, are a powerful tool for real estate investors. A 1031 exchange swaps an ownership interest in one property for another, deferring your tax liability. This type of sale isn't applicable to homeowners buying and selling primary residences. In addition, following the Tax Cuts and Jobs Act, 1031 exchanges only apply to real property, meaning vehicles, machinery, and other assets are ineligible for this type of tax treatment.[20] Here are the qualification criteria for a 1031 exchange:[21]

---

[19] Kelleher, Susan. "When Is the Best Time to Sell A House?" *Zillow*, 3 Nov 2024, https://www.zillow.com/learn/best-time-to-sell/.
[20] Internal Revenue Service. "Like-kind exchanges – Real estate tax tips." *Internal Revenue Service*, 9 Oct 2024, https://www.irs.gov/businesses/small-businesses-self-employed/like-kind-exchanges-real-estate-tax-tips.
[21] Hart, Dana. "Like-kind exchanges of real property." *Journal of Accountancy*, 1 Jan 2022, https://www.journalofaccountancy.com/issues/2022/jan/like-kind-exchanges-real-property.html.

- The property must be exchanged for a similar property. For example, a rental property for another rental property.
- A replacement property must be identified within 45 days of the date of the original sale.
- The replacement property must be acquired within 180 days of the date of the original sale.
- If the 1031 exchange has not been completed by the due date of the tax return (April 15th), an extension must be filed to preserve the 180-day exchange period. If no extension is filed, the 180-day exchange period ends on the due date of the return, triggering taxes on the sale.
- A Qualified Intermediary must be used to facilitate the exchange. This person must be independent.
- Property in the United States can only be exchanged for other property in the United States. For example, you can't sell a property in Texas and buy a property in Mexico.
- Form 8824 must be attached to your tax return, reporting the transaction.

Why go through the hassle of using a 1031 exchange? The main reason that real estate investors pursue 1031 exchanges is to defer taxes associated with property sales. Let's say that you meet the qualification criteria for a 1031 exchange. The property you are selling comes with a gain of $250,000. Assuming a 20% capital gains tax rate, you would be paying $50,000 in taxes in the year of the sale. Now, let's say you put the money directly into a new property. Now, you can defer the $50,000 tax liability until you sell the new property.

It's important to note that your depreciation expense on the new property will be lower. Using our above example, let's say the new property you're purchasing costs $400,000. Assuming no land is factored into the $400,000, your depreciable base drops to $150,000. This is found by subtracting your gain on sale from your new depreciable base.

Sounds simple, right? Well, not so fast. If the new property you're purchasing costs less than your gain on sale, depreciation recapture is triggered. Depreciation is recaptured up to the value of the depreciable property acquired. Let's say that the property you are selling had $50,000 in depreciation taken. The depreciable property in the new building is $25,000 less, subjecting $25,000 to depreciation recapture. Even if you purchase a new property worth more, you can still face depreciation recapture if the depreciable property is less than the property you're selling.

Installment Sales

Like 1031 exchanges, installment sales are another option to defer your tax liability associated with a property sale. This method can be used by both homeowners and real estate investors to spread out the gain of a property sale over multiple years. An installment sale, also known as seller financing, puts you in the shoes of a lender. Every month, or on a set schedule, you will receive payments from the buyer, which include both principal and interest payments. Homeowners who qualify for the homeowner exclusion can still have an installment sale without losing the exclusion.[22]

[22] Internal Revenue Service. "Topic no. 701, Sale of your home." *Internal Revenue Service,* 27 Sep 2024, https://www.irs.gov/taxtopics/tc701#:~:text=If%20you%20have%20an%20installment,under%20Section%20121%20remains%20available.

Unlike a 1031 exchange, installment sales have flexibility in how they're structured. For example, you can choose to be repaid over two years or ten. Although you can choose the interest rate, setting it near the market rate is important. For example, if current interest rates are 8% and you set a rate of 1%, it might raise red flags at the IRS. A rate between 4% and 6% would be reasonable based on a market rate of 8%. It's important to note that a sale is considered an installment sale if at least one payment is received in a different tax year. For example, if you have seven payments in one year and five in the next, the IRS considers the transaction an installment sale.

One of the main benefits of an installment sale is the ability to spread gains on the sale across multiple tax years. Let's say that you sell a property for $500,000 and your basis after closing costs is $300,000. This generates a taxable gain of $200,000. You decide to do an installment sale over ten years with a $100,000 down payment at a 5% interest rate. What does this look like over the first 12-month period?

- Monthly Payments - $4,243 ($50,916 over 12 months)
- Interest Paid - $19,282
- Gain - $20,000

Instead of picking up the full $200,000 gain in the year of the sale, you will report $20,000 each year. This has the potential to put you in a lower capital gains tax bracket. However, the interest income you earn is also taxable in the year earned. In our above example, you would report $19,282 of interest income on your tax return in the first year.

Remember our friend depreciation recapture? Well, you can't avoid this tax when using an installment sale. Taxes related to depreciation recapture are due in the year of the sale, regardless of whether you are using the installment sale method. Nevertheless, installment sales can be a great strategy to increase your sale price, earn additional interest income, and lower your capital gains taxes.

Sales Within Tax-Advantaged Accounts

Holding property in a tax-advantaged account is another popular strategy for minimizing taxes on your real estate sales. If you hold the property in a self-directed IRA, any gain on sale will not be taxed. Funds are only taxed when withdrawals are made from a pre-tax account. If the property is owned through a Roth, the gain on sale can grow tax-free or be applied to your next purchase without any tax implications. When using tax-advantaged accounts, consulting with an accountant or a qualified financial advisor is always best.

Interest Rate Implications for Sellers

Sellers also need to be aware of interest rate implications. A rate of 8% can yield drastically different results compared to a rate of 5%. In this section, we'll cover what to expect when selling a property with high rates versus low rates.

High Rates

High rates mean lower buyer demand. Fewer buyers are willing to take on a mortgage with higher interest rates, making it common for properties to sit on the market longer. In order to sell your property, you may need to accept a lower price. If your property is not selling for your ideal price, consider converting it into a rental unit. Otherwise, be prepared to haggle with buyers on the purchase price and terms.

Low Rates

When rates are low, you'll notice more buyer demand. This is because buyers are able to qualify for loans with more ease. As more buyers enter the market, home prices are driven up, helping you secure top-dollar for your home. However, your potential tax liability will also increase when sale prices increase. A $50,000 difference in the sale price of your home could mean a higher capital gains tax bracket and potentially cause you to exceed the homeowner exclusion amount if you are selling a primary home.

Low rates also mean you have more opportunities to hold onto properties. Instead of selling the property and paying higher capital gains tax rates, you can refinance it at a lower rate. A smaller monthly payment might make the property an ideal rental. If you're considering this situation, run the numbers and work with a leasing agent to understand the tentative rent before moving forward.

Conclusion

Are you ready to list your property for sale? Remember, the tax code and the real estate market are always changing, making it important to work closely with industry professionals to maximize compliance and minimize your tax burden. Countless homeowners and real estate investors find selling property daunting because of capital gains taxes. However, armed with the right strategies, you can walk out ahead. In the next section, we'll cover special situations you might come across, including dealing with inherited property, the taxation of second homes, and specific tax implications for real estate investors.

Part 3: Special Situations

Transacting with real property isn't always as simple as buying and selling. In fact, there can be special circumstances surrounding the sale that impact your taxation. That's exactly what we'll cover in this section. First, we'll start with a discussion on foreclosures and short sales. Oftentimes, these sales come with adverse tax implications, especially when you buy and sell within a 12-month period.

Then, we'll move on to inherited and gifted property, including how you calculate your basis, which ownership types receive a step-up in basis, and the implications of giving property as a gift. Next, we'll outline important tax considerations when owning a second home or vacation property. You might be surprised at the deductions and credits you can claim.

Finally, we'll end this section with an in-depth discussion of various tax implications for real estate investors. By now, you should understand that the IRS has special rules for real estate professionals, many of which are beneficial. These one-off situations occur more than you might think, so let's dive in!

Foreclosures and Short Sales

Remember our discussion on the 2008 Mortgage Crisis? Real estate can be a great way to build wealth; however, it isn't foolproof. The market can take a downturn, your lender might call your mortgage due, or you may have simply overleveraged. Each of these situations can result in foreclosures and short sales. Let's explore the potential tax consequences of these two situations in more detail.

Foreclosures

When a third party (usually a lender) wants to recoup a portion of their money, they will start the foreclosure process. Ownership rights are transferred to your lender, allowing them to sell the property. Two situations can occur:

1. The lender sells your property for more than you owe. You will receive the excess funds after the loan balance and closing costs are subtracted.
2. The lender sells your property for less than you owe. You will be required to make the lender "whole" by repaying any remaining loan balance.

The foreclosure or repossession of a property is treated the same way as a normal sale, requiring reporting on Schedule D. The same rules for primary residences also apply. You can claim the homeowner exclusion if you qualify, but no losses on the sale are deductible. For real estate investors, losses are deductible.[23]

Short Sales

A short sale occurs when you buy and sell your home within a short amount of time (generally within a 12-month period). Short sales are taxed as short-term capital gains, subjecting any gain to ordinary income tax instead of preferential long-term capital gains rates. In addition, short sales will not meet the requirements for the homeowner exclusion, subjecting gains from the sale of a primary home held for under 12 months to ordinary income taxes. However, losses are not deductible on primary residences unless you convert the property to a rental prior to the sale.

Inherited or Gifted Property

Whether you are setting up how your real estate will be disbursed upon your death or have received or inherited property, it's important to understand the tax implications. Both inherited and gifted property will be subject to taxation on the difference between the gross sale price and your basis. Let's explore the rules for inherited and gifted property in more detail.

Inherited Property

Inherited property isn't taxed until sold. Determining the amount of inherited property subject to tax depends on your basis in the property, much like a traditional sale we discussed earlier. Upon death, two things can happen:

---

[23] Internal Revenue Service. "Foreclosures and Capital Gain or Loss." *Internal Revenue Service,* 2024, https://apps.irs.gov/app/vita/content/36/36_03_050.jsp.

1. <u>Step-Up in Basis</u> – Certain inherited property receives a step-up in basis. A step-up in basis adjusts the transferor's original basis amount to the fair market value on the date of death. Let's say your relative has a basis of $150,000 in a property. Upon their death, the appreciated fair market value is $350,000. Instead of retaining the $150,000 basis, you will use the stepped-up basis of $350,000 in your tax calculation.
2. <u>Retain Original Basis</u> – In certain situations, you will retain the basis of the transferor with no step-up. This can result in a higher tax burden for property that has significant appreciation.

So, how do you determine if you are eligible for a step-up in basis? Property held personally or through a disregarded entity automatically receives a step-up in basis upon death. Property held in a partnership doesn't automatically receive a step-up in basis but can elect a step-up in basis under Section 754. The same goes for S Corporations, although the process is more complex. C Corporations do not receive a step-up in basis; however, the value of the stock held in the C Corporation will receive a step-up. It's also important to note that property held in an irrevocable trust will not receive a step-up in basis.[24]

Gifted Property

Gifted property can come with tax implications for both the recipient and the person issuing the gift. When you receive a gift, you are awarded the donor's basis in the property. However, if the donor pays gift tax on the appreciated value of the property, you will receive a step-up in basis. Let's say that your grandfather gifts you a property worth $500,000. His original basis is $300,000. If he pays gift tax on the $200,000 of appreciation, you will receive a step-up in basis. If no gift tax is paid, your basis will remain at $300,000. When you sell the property, any gain in excess of your adjusted basis will be subject to taxes, unless you qualify for the homeowner exclusion.

Gifted property also draws in the lifetime gift tax exclusion. The 2025 lifetime gift tax exclusion is currently set at $13.99 million per individual. Like many other provisions of the 2017 Tax Cuts and Jobs Act, the lifetime gift tax exclusion is set to revert back down to $7 million starting in 2026. It's also important to note that a gift tax return is required when you gift property worth more than $19,000 in 2025. Although you will not pay taxes if you are under the lifetime exclusion, you still need to report the transaction to the IRS by filing Form 709.[25]

Owning a Second Home or Vacation Property

Owning a second home or vacation property comes with additional tax considerations. For one, if you use the property solely for your personal use, refer to our deductions and credits section in Part 1 for an in-depth explanation of what's deductible and eligible. Generally, you can deduct all the same items as your primary home.

---

[24] Internal Revenue Service. "Gifts & Inheritances." *Internal Revenue Service,* 10 Oct 2024, https://www.irs.gov/faqs/interest-dividends-other-types-of-income/gifts-inheritances/gifts-inheritances.
[25] Internal Revenue Service. "Frequently asked questions on gift taxes." *Internal Revenue Service,* 29 Oct 2024, https://www.irs.gov/businesses/small-businesses-self-employed/frequently-asked-questions-on-gift-taxes.

However, if you are using a second home or vacation property to generate rental income, there are specific rules you need to follow. First, if you rent your property for 14 days or less, you aren't required to report rental income under the Augusta Rule. This rule is designed to avoid the hassle of reporting rental income and expenses for taxpayers with minimal rental days.[26]

For example, if your business rents your beach house in Florida one week out of the year or you live near a popular event and Airbnb your home for a few days, you do not need to file Schedule E on your return. This also means rental expenses related to that timeframe are not deductible.

Once you exceed 14 days, you are required to file Schedule E and report income and expenses. However, you are only able to deduct expenses related to the days you generate income. For example, if you spend three months out of the year at your vacation home and rent it out for the remaining nine months, you will only be able to deduct 75% of property taxes, insurance, and mortgage interest. You are able to deduct the full amount of expenses incurred during those nine months, including utility bills, repairs, maintenance, and supplies. Personal use expenses must be excluded.

Tax Implications for Real Estate Investors

This section is dedicated to real estate investors. Even if you don't currently own investment properties, this section can still be helpful. In addition to all of the above information we've covered, real estate investors have a few more tax regulations they need to understand. In this section, we'll cover four main things: passive activity loss rules, real estate professional status, short-term rental regulations, and special depreciation options.

Passive Activity Loss Rules

Passive real estate losses may be limited on your individual income tax return. According to the IRS, there are two kinds of passive activities:[27]

1. A trade or business that you don't materially participate in during the year.
2. Rental activities with material participation but no real estate professional status.

If either of these factors is true, the losses generated will be limited; however, losses can be used to offset other passive income. Let's say that your real estate activities are considered passive. One property generates $10,000 of income, while another property sustains a $15,000 loss. In the current year, you will be able to use up to $10,000 of the loss to offset your $10,000 of income. The remaining amount will be carried forward to offset future passive income.

There is a special $25,000 passive activity loss allowance for passive real estate if you have a modified adjusted gross income below a certain threshold. For the 2023 tax year, this threshold is $100,000. The special allowance is reduced by 50% of your modified adjusted gross income above

---

[26] Internal Revenue Service. "Topic no. 415, Renting residential and vacation property." *Internal Revenue Service*, 20 Aug 2024, https://www.irs.gov/taxtopics/tc415.

[27] Internal Revenue Service. "Publication 925 (2023), Passive Activity and At-Risk Rules." *Internal Revenue Service*, 9 Sep 2024, https://www.irs.gov/publications/p925.

$100,000, up to $150,000. Let's say that your adjusted gross income is $120,000. Here's how you would calculate your special allowance:

1. Subtract income in excess of the base threshold ($120,000 - $100,000)
2. Multiply the result by 50% ($20,000 x 50%)
3. Subtract the result from $25,000 allowance ($25,000 - $10,000)

In the above scenario, you could deduct up to $15,000 of passive real estate losses. Any losses in excess of this amount are carried forward to future years. Passive activity losses from real estate don't apply if you are considered a real estate professional, which is what we'll discuss in the next section.

Real Estate Professional Status

Real estate activities are generally considered passive, even if you materially participate. However, if you qualify as a real estate professional, your rental activity is considered active income, not passive. To qualify as a real estate professional, you must meet both of the following requirements:[28]

1. More than half of the professional services you performed during the year were related to real estate activities that you materially participated in.
2. You performed more than 750 service hours during the year related to real estate.

It's important to note that your services don't have to be solely related to running rental properties. Working as a realtor, cleaning real estate apartments, marketing for a real estate agency, and lending activities are all considered real estate activities. When you meet the requirements for real estate professional status, your rental activities are considered active income. This means you can deduct all losses without being limited to passive activity loss rules.

Let's say that you have W-2 income of $75,000 during the year. You also qualify for real estate professional status and report a $30,000 loss from your rental activities. Since your rental activities are considered active income, you are able to deduct the entire $30,000 loss on your income tax return. If you did not qualify for real estate professional status, your loss would be limited.

Short-Term Rental Regulations

Short-term and long-term rentals are treated differently in the eyes of the IRS. Long-term rentals are reported on Schedule E, while some short-term rentals may qualify for Schedule C treatment. Schedule C is used to report rental expenses when you provide substantial services for the tenant's convenience, such as regular cleanings.[29]

For many short-term rental hosts, this is the case. If your property is listed on websites like Airbnb and Vrbo and generally has stays that average less than 30 days, your rental activity should be

---

[28] Internal Revenue Service. "Publication 925 (2023), Passive Activity and At-Risk Rules." *Internal Revenue Service,* 9 Sep 2024, https://www.irs.gov/publications/p925.
[29] Internal Revenue Service. "Publication 527 (2024), Residential Rental property." *Internal Revenue Service,* 24 Dec 2024, https://www.irs.gov/publications/p527#en_US_2024_publink1000234064.

reported on Schedule C. The advantage of this is the ability to bypass passive activity loss limitations because your rental activity is considered active income.

Special Depreciation Options

Earlier in this book, we alluded to special depreciation options. In this section, we'll dive into the two main types of special depreciation options: Section 179 and Bonus Depreciation. As you read through this section, remember that the allowability of these special depreciation options can vary by state. Some states will allow Section 179 but not Bonus, making it important to consult with a tax accountant.

Section 179

Section 179 allows you to immediately expense the cost of an asset placed in service before the end of the year. Generally, assets are required to be depreciated over their useful life. However, this depreciation deduction allows you to expedite the deduction of certain qualifying assets. Section 179 cannot create a loss, but it can reduce your income down to zero.

Bonus Depreciation

The second type of special depreciation option is Bonus Depreciation. Bonus Depreciation is set to phase out under the 2017 Tax Cuts and Jobs Act. However, you can still take a 60% deduction for eligible assets. Unlike Section 179, Bonus Depreciation can create a loss on your tax return. Let's say you have an income of $50,000 and assets that cost $60,000, all of which are eligible for Bonus Depreciation. You can generate a $10,000 loss with Bonus Depreciation.

Cost Segregation Studies

Both Section 179 and Bonus Depreciation only apply to certain assets. The building itself is specifically excluded from eligibility. This is where cost segregation studies come into play, helping you pick out eligible assets from the building itself. Let's say that you purchase a property for $200,000. Assuming no land value, you would be required to depreciate the building over its useful life, which can either be 27.5 years for residential or 39 years for commercial.

Instead of depreciating the full $200,000 over its useful life, you can get a cost segregation study done. This study will assign a value to the different components of the building. For example, the roof might be worth $25,000, while the windows are worth $10,000. Breaking these items out allows you to leverage special depreciation options to take a larger upfront deduction. If you are planning on pursuing a cost segregation study, it does need to be done by a professional.

Part 4: Planning Ahead

Real estate isn't a set-it-and-forget-it strategy, especially for investors. In fact, maximizing your real estate gains and minimizing your tax liability can take five to ten years of planning. Although there's no telling what the future might hold, the best real estate investors and homeowners take the time to look ahead and create a strategy.

First, we'll cover when you might want to change your business structure from a disregarded entity to a 1065 or 1120s. Changing business structures also means changes in your taxes, which can be more favorable. Then, we'll dive into when it's time to consult with a tax professional. Hint: It's always best to consult a tax professional before buying your first property. Our final section will touch on succession planning, including the implications of trusts and estates. This part will be short and sweet, covering the fundamentals of planning ahead you need to know.

Switching Business Structures

Throughout this book, we've discussed the tax implications of real estate transactions on your income tax return. For homeowners, most real estate transactions will be made on their personal returns since the IRS considers the home personal property. However, real estate investors have flexibility in how they report their transactions.

Most novice real estate investors will start as a disregarded entity, which is either a sole proprietorship or a single-member LLC structure. As you begin to add properties or take on new investors, it can be beneficial to change your business type. You can consider switching to two main structures: a Partnership or an S Corporation. Let's break down the fundamentals of each business type, including the pros and cons.

Partnership

A Partnership is a legally separate business with two or more partners. Profit and loss are split according to a partnership agreement. For example, if the profit split is 60/40 and there is $100,000 of profit for the year, Partner A would receive $60,000, and Partner B would receive $40,000. All income or loss in a Partnership is pass-through, meaning it's reported and taxed on your individual income tax return. The main advantage of a Partnership is the ability to snowball your deals. After all, you have more resources coming to the table. In addition, in a Partnership, you also share liabilities, reducing risks.

One disadvantage of a Partnership is an increase in reporting obligations. Partnerships must file a separate business tax return each year. Additionally, a portion of the Partnership income might still be subject to self-employment taxes. Another disadvantage is the diluted ownership percentage. You can't solely decide to buy or sell a property. You need the approval of other partners. Partner approval also applies to distributions and contributions.

S Corporation

An S Corporation is a Limited Liability Company that elects to be taxed as a Corporation. S Corporations work similarly to Partnerships, with all income or loss flowing through to your individual income tax return. One of the main advantages of an S Corporation is avoiding self-employment taxes on earnings. However, the IRS does require S Corporation owners to pay themselves a reasonable salary with payroll taxes imposed.

S Corporations will need to file a separate business tax return each year, making it more expensive to maintain. However, the ability to safeguard a portion of your profit and loss from self-employment taxes offers an advantageous tax planning situation. S Corporations also make it easy to change ownership, giving you flexibility when you need to bring on another investor. Like Partnerships, bringing on additional owners can dilute your ownership percentage.

Is It Time to Switch?

There's no one-size-fits-all answer on when it's time to switch your business structure; however, there are some indicators:

- You want to partner with investors by offering ownership of a property.
- Your self-employment tax obligations continue to grow.
- You want a step-up in basis if a partner does pass.

Before you change your business structure, it's important to be aware of adverse tax implications. For one, you cannot have a Partnership with only one partner. Partnerships need to have at least two partners. If you plan on bringing a partner on short-term, you may want to consider an alternative structure. Similarly, transferring mortgaged property into an S Corporation can trigger a taxable gain. These examples aren't meant to scare you away but to make you aware of potential adverse tax implications, which is why it's best to consult with a tax accountant before making any decisions.

When It's Time to Consult a Tax Professional

We alluded to the importance of consulting with a tax professional in the previous section. In this section, we'll expand on the vital role a tax professional plays when it comes to managing and reporting your real estate activities.

The Services Tax Professionals Offer

Each tax professional will offer a different set of services. Nevertheless, here are some basic services you can expect from a tax professional:

- Transaction management and bookkeeping
- Tax planning and estimate preparation
- Fixed asset management and depreciation calculations
- Representation in audits and inquiries
- Tax preparation
- Deduction and credit maximization
- Advice on timing sales and purchases
- Compilations, reviews, and audits
- Cash flow and general business consulting
- Entity structure advice

Each of these services can help you bolster your compliance with the IRS, maximize your profit margins, and minimize your tax liability.

The Benefits of Working with a Tax Professional

While it might be difficult to see the benefits a tax professional can offer, they are there. Here are a few of the main benefits of contracting a tax professional to help with your real estate tax reporting:

- Leverages all available real estate tax credits and deductions to lower taxable income.
- Avoids costly mistakes and errors with returns filed with the IRS and state agencies.

- Provides tax knowledge and advice on how to minimize your tax liability.
- Saves you valuable time preparing tax returns and other filings.
- Helps you lower your audit risk and ensure compliance with applicable tax laws.
- Assists with tax planning and estimate preparation to go into filing season prepared.
- Gives you peace of mind that all obligations are properly taken care of.
- Represents you in an audit or inquiry with backed data and support.

Not only do most real estate investors and homeowners save money by working with a tax accountant, but they also have less stress surrounding their reporting.

When It's Time to Bring in a Tax Professional

Is it time for you to bring in a tax professional? Even if your real estate transactions aren't complicated, working with a tax professional is always advised. Here are some instances when it's highly recommended to consult with a tax accountant:

- You are preparing to get pre-approved for a home loan. A tax accountant can ensure your return is fully compliant, reducing lender questions.
- You own a home and want to maximize your deduction and credits.
- You own investment property.
- You own a second home or vacation rental with personal use.
- You are considering a short-term rental business.
- You have other forms of income, like W-2 or 1099 income, and want to leverage real estate losses.
- You are considering selling a property.
- You engaged in a 1031 exchange.
- You are selling a property over the span of multiple years.
- You want to purchase real estate through an IRA.
- You want to grow your real estate empire without overpaying on taxes.
- You need quarterly estimates to cover your real estate income.
- You want more insights into your tax liability throughout the year.
- You find yourself stressing about taxes throughout the year.
- You make energy-efficient home improvements.

Every type of real estate transaction can warrant professional tax advice. Even if you don't currently have any real estate, consult with an accountant! Having a trusted team member by your side is especially important if you plan on growing your investments.

Succession Planning

Although we all wish we could live forever, the reality is that one day we will pass. Ensuring your succession plan properly accounts for your real estate can avoid probate court, family disputes, and costly legal fees. You can protect your real estate in countless ways, but the most common are trusts and wills.

A will outlines how you want your assets disbursed upon your passing. In most cases, property will first default to your surviving spouse. Then, after your spouse passes, it will be distributed to beneficiaries of your choosing. Without a legal document in place, your real estate interests could go to someone you may not want. For example, many states will distribute everything to your children, even if you have no relationship. This is why it's critical that you have the necessary legal documents in place to carry out your directives.

The process can be more complex for real estate professionals, especially for appreciated property. If you remember back to our section about basis step-ups, you want to be sure that your beneficiaries minimize their tax burden. Having a robust succession plan in place is beneficial, even if you are young and active. You never know what life will throw at you. For more information on succession planning, reach out to an attorney well-versed in real estate, and always consult with a tax accountant.

Part 5: Resources and Tools

By now, we should have dispelled many of the myths and misconceptions associated with real estate transactions. However, your learning doesn't have to stop here. Our book covered the basic principles you'll come across, but it isn't a tell-all of every situation you'll encounter. This makes it essential that you continue your learning in areas that are prevalent to your real estate holdings. In this section, we'll quickly outline some of our favorite resources and tools that you can utilize to expand your knowledge.

Recommended Books

- Every Landlord's Tax Deduction Guide by Stephen Fishman J.D.
- The Book on Advanced Tax Strategies by Amanda Han and Matthew MacFarland
- The Book on Advanced Tax Strategies for the Savvy Real Estate Investor by Amanda Han and Matthew MacFarland
- Advanced Tax Strategies for High Income Earners by Jorge Ospina
- Tax-Free Wealth by Tom Wheelwright

Helpful Tools

- Amortization Calculator - https://www.calculator.net/amortization-calculator.html
- Interest Rate Index - https://www.mortgagenewsdaily.com/mortgage-rates/mnd

Our Contact Information

- Website: www.BCMFirm.com
- Email: Brad@BCMFirm.com
- Direct number: (832) 971-4355
- Office number: (713) 213-7631

Conclusion

The purpose of this book was to dispel any misconceptions associated with buying and selling real estate, regardless of whether you are investing in real estate for personal use or to build a business. In Part 1, we took a deep dive into the tax implications of buying real estate, including the importance of filing income tax returns, tax deductions and credits you may be eligible to claim, how closing costs are treated, tax planning strategies, and interest rate implications.

In Part 2, we laid out the opposite: the tax implications of selling real estate. Here, we discussed which selling expenses are eligible for a deduction, capital gains taxes and other taxes you might come across, how to report the sale of your property, tax planning strategies for selling real estate, and interest rate implications for sellers.

Part 3 was our catch-all section, where we covered special situations, including foreclosures, short sales, inherited and gifted property, and second homes. We also outlined tax implications for real estate investors, like passive activity loss limitations, the tax treatment of short-term rentals, and special depreciation options.

Part 4 provided indicators on when it's time to contact a professional and the benefits a tax accountant can provide, such as minimizing your tax liability and ensuring compliance with the IRS and state agencies. Finally, Part 5 provided resources and tools to continue learning about real estate.

By now, you should have an overview of the major tax implications associated with your real estate transactions. However, this book isn't a substitute for professional advice. If you have any questions on the tax or accounting specifics of your real estate transactions, reach out to our team today.

Bradford C. Moye, CPA - Attorney at Law
Bradford C. Moye, PLLC
Brad@BCMFirm.com
www.BCMFirm.com